My Book of Rhymes

Joy Elaine Zaleski

PublishAmerica

Baltimore

First printing

ISBN: 1-4241-1850-6
PUBLISHED BY PUBLISHAMERICA, LLLP
www.publishamerica.com
Baltimore

Printed in the United States of America

Dedication:

This book is dedicated to my brothers and sisters, who first taught me about love. To my daughters, Tami Gorup Hawkins, Tina (Tia) Gorup and Eileen Zaleski, and my son Edward Zaleski III and his wife, Lori, who continue to bless me with their love. To my grandchildren, Aubri, Rodney, Alan, Morgan, Cassondra, Edward IV, and my great-granddaughter, Hannah, who have always shown me unconditional love. Without love, there is no life.

I dedicate my poem "Hometown Boy" to the memory of USMC Cpl. Ian Zook of Port St. Lucie, Florida, who was killed in Iraq on October 12, 2004.

Acknowledgments:

To my daughter Eileen Zaleski, I offer my most heartfelt love and appreciation for her knowledge, labor and expertise in helping me get this work to the publisher. Without her, it simply would not have happened.

A special thank you to Hannah Mackenzie Morris, my five-year-old, great-granddaughter, who cheerfully contributed the art work. Hannah is the daughter of Rodney and Aubri Morris and attends St. Anastasia School in Ft. Pierce, Florida.

To my dear friends Noilly Turley and Lynn Oppenheimer, and so many others, I thank you from the bottom of my heart for your love, support and encouragement.

To my deceased daughter Tami, thank you for being in my life. I wish you could have stayed.

Photograph provided by Kim Jacobus of Port St. Lucie, Florida.

Table of Contents

I Have An Angel

I have an angel who watches over me.
I know she's there. I know she can see.

She's always with me when I'm happy or I'm sad.
She's always with me when I'm good or I'm bad

I feel her presence all around.
Whether I'm feeling up, or really down.

When I am frightened. Strange sounds in the night.
She is there. Calming my unknown fright.

When I have dreams that I can't seem to make sense of,
My angel comforts me with thoughts of her love.

It makes me feel better, just knowing she's there.
She makes the hard times a lot easier to bear.

The glad times are always a wonderful treat.
She keeps me happy. Gives me dancing feet!

I have an angel who watches over me.
I know she's there. I know she can see.

The Glory of Spring

As the leaves turn green, in the early spring,
Before the hard ground is warm.
Crocuses peek through the pockets of snow,
Demanding their place in the sun.

Every small bud on the bush, will soon bloom.
Flowers will dance in the breeze.
Gardens will pop up all over the town,
Heavenly scents beckon bees.

Islands of daffodils, will bow their heads,
Just as Spring Maidens go by.
Kissing bluebirds, assembling their nests,
Lovingly soar to the sky.

Maple trees donating all of their sap,
Nary a moment too soon.
Outdoor pots, cooking over hot fires.
Pancake syrup, before noon.

Quiet days of winter, now are waning.
Relegated to the past.
Spring in all its glory has come this day.
To the heavens, eyes are cast.

Up to God, we sing our praises loud.
Views of a wonderful scene.
Why would we want to be anywhere else?
Xanthippe would be serene.

Yesterday dreary clouds were mostly gray,
Zing! Suddenly it's Spring! It's here to stay.

Note: This poem is written with each line beginning with the
next consecutive letter of the alphabet. It was a challenge by
my poetry group and fun to do!

Photographs

We are surrounded by photographs of family and friends.
They seem to keep life in a circle, without any ends.

I know I am never alone. Have no reason to feel sad.
I just look at my photographs, and my heart feels glad.

Like the hugs I've received from those I love,
Always seem to remind me of the love from above.

I can see the little ones grow, from one year to another.
See the smiles on the faces of their father and mother.

I share in the excitement of their first prom.
Expressions on their faces. Trying to act so calm.

Pictures of ball games, parties and sports,
Of lovely young ladies in very short shorts!

Snapshots of young men, going off to school.
At times giving impressions of not being so cool!

Tears spring to my eyes, sometimes blurring my sight,
When I think of the prayers I've said every night.

The prayers have been answered. I never had doubt.
I've always known, just how it would turn out.

I can go through my days, with a song in my heart.
Photographs keep them close. We're never far apart.

Moments of Bliss

As I sit here aging in my oasis of sun,
Thoughts come to me of how my life had begun.

I can see in my memory of the very early years,
I was about four. I had no fears.

Mother is hanging a wash. Colors and whites.
Sheets flapping in the breeze like flying kites.

Easter baskets filled with decorated eggs.
Hidden so well, it seemed they had legs.

Summer rains. Thunder and lightning flashing.
Mother beckoning me to her side. The rain splashing.

The fall of the year. Leaves drifting to the ground.
All the colors of autumn. Waiting to be found.

Winter comes along. Jack Frost etches the glass.
Christmas! A wonderful time! Midnight Mass.

Snowmen standing in the front yard.
Ever protective. Always on guard.

Colds and fevers and sometimes the flu.
Mother always seemed to know what to do.

A nice warm bath. Vicks rubbed on my chest.
Tucked into bed. Mother does know best.

Up in the morning, feeling fresh and cool,
The real awakening, it's time for school!

These days are remembered. Moments of bliss,
One thing lacking. Mother's sweet kiss.

The Dandelion

Once, many years ago, when I was just a little one,
I arose on Mother's Day morning. Went out into the sun.

Our front yard sparkled with the drippings of dew,
But, was also engulfed in a lovely yellow hue.

I began picking those beautiful little blooms,
Knowing they would brighten our drab, small rooms.

Mother chose our only vase. Very fine cut glass.
She stood the blossoms in it, with a little grass.

We set the beautiful arrangement on our windowsill.
As I think back about it right now, I can see it still.

She smiled as neighbors commented on the array.
My heart was warmed forever, that lovely day in May.

Some may think of the dandelion as a lowly weed.
But, to me, it's another of God's blessings, indeed.

The Ballerina

She dreamed of becoming a ballerina. Practiced her art every day.
But, her father forbad her to pursue it. She was brought up to obey.
She married, and had many children at a very early age.
Her dreams went into an old trunk. She would never be on stage.

She raised her children in a loving home. Made their lives a living joy.
She encouraged her children to chase their dreams. Each girl, and every boy.
The children grew up. Some went to college. Others got good jobs, and were wed.
They taught their children to follow their hearts. Recalling what their mother had said.

Days turned into years, as time went by. Families were doing fine.
But their mother was having problems. Thought she was losing her mind.
She would place the milk in the cupboard. The bread often into the oven.
And though she didn't always know them. She still gave her children her lovin'.

They noticed that she couldn't dress herself. Turned the air on, when it was cold.
Didn't take her medicine as prescribed. They thought she was just getting old.

They wondered what was going on in her mind. Is she still able to dream?
She wanted so much to be a ballerina. Does she still have a gleam?

Then she began to wander and to roam. Her children had a gnawing fear.
Sadly, they chose to place her in a home. Her thoughts just weren't very clear.
It's hard to watch her drift slowly away. They remembered the good times so clearly.
But, at least they know she'll be well taken care of. This mother they loved so dearly.

They'd visit her as often as they could, though she no longer knew their names.
They'd sit by her bed for hours, talking cheerfully. Not one of their favorite games.
Now the end of her days is drawing near. All that is left is to pray.
They hoped she'd found happiness in her life. Her life had been their ballet.

What I Really Meant To Say

I can't remember if I ever told you,
What loving you has meant.
How when I was just a little girl,
I loved to smell your scent.

How I loved your big brown eyes,
When you looked at me.
And how the sound of your voice,
Made me think of a melody.

And the way you piled your hair,
On top of your head, or curled.
And how just one big smile from you,
Would really light up my world.

The way you shared the secrets of
A beautiful day in spring.
And the quiet times, as we listened
to a songbird sing.

The times you let me play dress-up,
In your clothes and dressy shoes.
And when I played a game,
You taught me how to win, or lose.

You sent me off to school each day,
With a shining, happy face.
And you always encouraged me,
To run a fair and honest race.

I wish I had told you how much
These things had meant to me.
And I would want you to know,
In my life, your love had been the key.

I miss you so much, Mom.
I wish you were here today,
So I could finally tell you all the things,
That I really meant to say.

What Feeds My Heart

So many things I want to say, but, it seems time gets in the way.
I hurry here, I hurry there. Before I know, it's the end of the day.

I go to bed, I need to sleep, then get back up because I can't.
Sleep won't come, I need to write, or at least I need to rant.

I saw an angel in the sky the other day. Well, actually a cloud.
But, it was in the shape of an angel. I said so, out loud.

I find myself looking up into the skies more and more.
I recall my mother doing the same thing. I tried to ignore.

I feel that I'm looking for answers, for questions I don't have.
I've always had faith in God. For this I've always been glad.

I've really had such a wonderful life. Broken heart, now and then.
But, everyone has some sadness and strife. It's a place we've all been.

It's all a part of living. Sunshine and rain. Happiness and pain.
We pick ourselves up, stick out our chin. Begin all over again.

I've always believed in tomorrow. Looked for the sun after a rain.
Looked for rainbows. Blue skies. Knew there'd be an end to the pain.

And there always was. Something would happen to brighten the day.
A new baby. A note from an old friend. "I love you," someone would say.

I don't know what makes some people give up, and others just plod along.
I wish I could bottle what feeds my heart. Give someone a happy song.

All I can do is give a hug and a smile. And try to listen with my heart.
And somehow let them know, that tomorrow is a brand new start.

God gave us our days in minutes and hours. He knew all about time.
He broke the days down to what we could handle. Grapes on a vine.

We must learn to wait until just the right moment, to pick the sweetest yield.
If it's not today, then it must be tomorrow. And we'll find our heart has healed.

Moving Day

To my brother I say, it's been my pleasure to know you.
Though I haven't always taken the time to show you.
My memories of you go back a long way.
Including when we packed to go away that sad day.

Our tears we choked back, as we bid mom goodbye,
In fact, in our family there was not a dry eye.
Foster homes were the destination of the day,
We had no way of knowing how long we would stay.

Our parents could not afford the overhead of our keep,
So we were sent to another's house to eat and to sleep.
Two by two, like on the Ark, we were chosen to go.
But, the flood was our tears that did suddenly flow.

The treat to ride in a car, (meager belongings in a box),
Failed to ease our sad hearts, which were heavy as rocks.
The house we were sent to, was worse than we'd had.
The people looked kind, but in fact were very bad.

They beat the children, when no crime had been done.
Nothing children could do. No place to run.
We went to school, filthy dirty each morn,
Wondering as a child would, just why we were born.

Then one day, the Social Worker came to say,
Get your things together, you're going away.
Relieved to be leaving, but scared of the destination,
We looked out the car window, with little expectation.

They greeted us warmly, those two on a farm.
Like a Grandma and Grandpa, they meant us no harm.
We stayed there till Christmas, and then got the news,
We were going home. We even got new shoes!

Christmas Love

I've begun wrapping Christmas presents, for my family and friends.
It's something I enjoy doing, yet, it seems it never ends.

I remember when I was quite young, we were so very poor.
We did receive gifts, but of course, hoping for more.

The downtown lights were shining; Christmas trees all aglow.
While we kids tried to earn money, shoveling other people's snow.

We bought little presents for each other and trimmed the Christmas tree.
Which dad always bought on Christmas Eve. (It was almost free.)

We used to laugh at the twigs sticking out from that pine.
But, once the lights were on it, it really began to shine.

We covered it with icicles. That's when it began to shimmer.
And gave us the hope of Christmas. That first little glimmer.

We secretly wrapped the gifts we'd bought. Mostly socks and underwear.
But, we covered them lovingly, to show we did care.

We didn't have the best of wrappings. Not a ribbon or a bow.
We used the paper from the year before, it seemed to still have a glow.

When the little kids went to bed, we placed the gifts under the
tree.
Then we stood there for a moment, my brother and me.

We wished each other a Merry Christmas, with a hug and a
smile,
Knowing the kids would be up, in a very short while.

We looked in to see them, snuggled two and three to a bed.
Looking forward to Santa and his bountiful sled.

We woke up early on Christmas morning, outside it wasn't
even light.
But, in our living room, that little tree stood all a glow and so
bright.

The kids were squealing. So very happy they were.
Santa had left a gift for each. He really had been there!

So as I wrap this mountain of gifts, I remember when,
A little family was happy with one gift each, way back then.

A Straight Mile

It was wonderful visiting with my brother and his wife.
Seems when we get together, we always discuss our life.

And discuss it we did, with a little joy and some sadness.
Culminating with great thanks for all of the gladness.

We realize that we had learned to look for the bright side.
That by living as we did, we can now look at the light side.

We can laugh at the antics of my brother as he grew,
As we learned the importance of being a family crew.

As youngsters, we were part of an impoverished upbringing.
Wearing hand-me-downs, did not warrant much singing.

But, we learned that no matter the clothes that we wore.
In this life we'd been born to, we'd be adding much more.

Collecting empty soda bottles, and shoveling snow,
Taught us that we wanted to be able to garner much more.

Graduating from high school. Getting a good job.
It was our battle cry. Set us apart from the mob.

We will always be thankful for the life we grew out of,
Knowing full well that God's plan, we never had doubt of.

We brothers and sisters are close to each other today.
We are profoundly grateful. It has helped pave our way.

Now our children and grandchildren are our blessings, so
sweet.
The joy of our lives, after the challenges, we did meet.

We are now much older. Can look back with a wry smile.
We did the best we could. We walked a straight mile.

Heart's Sweet Song

We spent the weekend together, my two sisters and I.
We talked and laughed and sometimes, had a little cry.

We used the time, talking of our lives and what they had meant.
And came to the conclusion, that ours had been heaven sent.

We also have dear brothers, whom we see once in a while.
Wish we could see them more often. They always make us smile.

We recalled that when we were young, we were very poor.
Quite often, we had to "borrow" sugar from next door.

Of course, it wasn't always sugar that we had to ask for.
Sometimes it was butter, or even bread, we had to implore.

We collected old soda bottles, found in other people's trash,
Which we carted to the grocery store for redemption of cash.

In winter, we'd shovel snow from other's driveways and walks,
In the evenings we'd make up games to play. Have serious talks.

Babysitting was a way to earn money for clothes and books.
We sisters had very little to spend on enhancing our looks.

But, we were happy and somewhat content with our impoverished lives.
Because we somehow knew that tomorrow brings hope, when it arrives.

We learned at an early age, to laugh, have fun and to share.
It was most important, to show each other that we care.

That we would always "be there" for each other. Good times or strife.
That God had a reason for bringing us together, in this instance of life.

I can't imagine how life would have been with any other.
We always were, to each of us, the other's mother.

It may sound odd to those who may read these words.
It proved to be our enrichment. Gave us wings, like a bird's.

So while we may talk of hardships in our days now long gone.
The love we have for each other, is ever our heart's sweet song.

Our Heart's Connection

I think of him often and wonder where he is today.
A lot of years have gone by, since he went away.

My life has changed so much, as lives are apt to do.
I know his must have changed in many ways, too.

I wonder if he's happy, as he's made his mark on life.
Or if instead, his world was continuously filled with strife.

He was such a gentle spirit. Hardly made a wave.
Just rolled with the punches. His own road he tried to pave.

School was not easy for him, in the early years.
But, steadfastly he moved along. Allaying any fears.

After graduation, he joined the Navy to see the world.
Met the girl of his dreams. Their wondrous life unfurled.

It seemed he'd found happiness, so illusive in his past.
But, then she died of a disease. It all happened so fast.

He raised his little boy, for a long while all alone.
Then met another girl, with which to make a home.

We've gone our separate ways, as some families do.
But, our heart's connection, is now and forever true.

I think of him often. Wonder where he is today.
My dear, gentle brother. I wish he'd never gone away.

Much More To Life

Do you ever feel blue? Feel that something is lacking?
I used to feel that way. But sent that feeling packing!

I was really quite young, when the thought occurred to me,
There was much more to life, than just the sadness I did see.

Being from a poor family, didn't help my self esteem.
But, being poor, gave me a lot of time to dream.

We didn't have the money to try to keep up a charade,
Instead, I spent a lot of time watching others parade.

I was able to learn a lot by watching and listening.
And soon realized that there wasn't much I was missing.

I had love all around me, from my sisters and brothers.
And soon felt the envy of the not-so-lucky others.

They expressed their jealousy, in quite a covert way,
Asking if they could come to our house, to have fun and play.

So whenever I feel blue, or that something is lacking,
I think of the "good" old days, and send that blueness packing!

We Lift Each Other

I can't imagine what my life would have been,
If not for my dear friends and each of my kin.

The memories we've made. The fun we've all had.
The times that we've shared the good, bad and sad

Those times when loved ones had to say goodbye.
Never quite ready, we tried not to cry.

Tears come to our eyes, as children leave the nest.
Some go off to school, striving to do their best.

Others join the Army, Navy and the Marines.
The urge to wander, inherent in their genes.

We lift each other up with a loving hand.
Knowing family and friends united will stand.

Life is a mixture of countless emotions.
Sometimes enough tears, to fill many oceans.

But, we've learned that even the worst of times will go.
That the sun will shine again. This we always do know.

Cutting the Umbilical Cord

Our children are older and now have children of their own.
But, we speak of them as though they still have not grown.

We worry about the things they do, and even what they say.
Truly try to cut the umbilical cord, every single day.

But, they are still our children, no matter what their ages.
If they do run amiss, we think of those times as stages

As though they will outgrow them, as they did their baby things.
We tend to forget that as they have grown, so have their wings.

It's hard for the mother bird to push her little ones from the nest.
But, she knows that once she's done it, it is for the best.

We forget that it's important, to let them find their own way.
To let them fall sometimes, so they'll appreciate a better day.

They don't learn from our experience, no matter how hard we try.
They need to do things for themselves, to really know how to fly.

So we must sit back sometimes and bite our tongues real hard.
Let them know we pray for them. But, they are their own guard.

And in knowing all of this, we as parents try to loosen our restrain.
Then along come grandchildren. We again sing the same old refrain.

Who Do They See?

She gazes at her offspring and then she sees their eyes.
They are looking back at her, but what do they surmise?

Do they see the little girl, who thought she'd be a queen?
Or perhaps the young lady, who had just turned sixteen.

Do they see the young woman, as she starts out in her life?
Or that very same woman, as she becomes a wife.

Do they know how it is to be their mother and grandmother?
That these dear babies were born to her, and not another?

Maybe they see the mom, who always listened as they spoke?
Who never treated their thoughts, as though they were a joke.

Do they see the grandma, who read them stories for many
hours?
And let them run barefooted, through sudden summer
showers.

Do they know this lady, and that she once had many dreams?
This older lady, who now sits and listens to their schemes.

Do they know how proud and happy she is on this very day?
Her children and grandchildren came into her heart to stay.

My Son

I dreamed of him, one night long ago.
He had blond curly hair, and a face all aglow.
I knew I would meet him sometime in my life.
I wasn't sure it would be as a mom or a wife.

But, as it turned out, he came as my son.
I knew when I saw him, that he was the one.
God had told me about him, many years before.
He knew I would welcome him to my door.

This son has been a blessing, right from the start.
He brought such happiness, to my life-weary heart.
He was beautiful of face. A smart little boy.
Every bit as nice. He brought unlimited joy.

As a teenager, he seemed to want only to please.
But, his unique sense of humor, labeled him a tease.
We'd stay up talking to the wee hours of morn,
Discussions ranging from wars, to why he was born.

They say a son is a son, till he takes a wife,
But, my son has been a good son, all of his life.
He calls to apologize for not calling before.
It's the sound of his voice, I deeply adore.

I know he's extremely busy, this son who's a dad,
The moments he spares me, make my heart glad.
I miss the talks, the kidding and the time.
But, the memories he created, are so sublime.

I'm very proud of how he has conducted his life,
And that he has a family, and a loving wife.
I wish him the happiness he has given me.
And all of the others, in our family tree.

My Daughters

My daughters, all lovely. I have only three.
They've brought a great quality of life to me.

Each one is different, as families go.
Usually warm as the sun. Rarely cold as the snow.

I'm proud of their accomplishments on this earth.
Their sense of family. Their knowledge of worth.

So much joy they've brought me through the years.
The times they made me laugh, even through my tears.

The blessings they gave me, with a cheery smile or a hug.
The glad memories we share. The sad times we try to shrug.

The notes and cards, throughout the years, they've sent,
Emotions of mine. Tears. The hankies they've lent.

I cannot imagine my life, without them in it.
Glad times, sad times. Wouldn't trade them for a minute.

They tug at my heartstrings, these daughters of mine,
Wish I could be with them, much longer than Time.

I fondly remember the phone in the closet. Guitar lessons.
Growth spurts.
I easily recall the good times. Choose to forget the "growing
up" hurts.

I've learned that a girl remains a daughter all of her life.
It makes no difference, whether she is, or isn't a wife.

There's a closeness. A bonding. No one else could understand.
It happens at birth, when you first hold that sweet hand.

I wish them happiness, good health and great love.
It comforts me to know, they have faith in God above.

We're each given blessings. To give life to our days.
Mine came as these daughters, who taught me their ways.

My Daughter, My Friend

My daughter sent me a Christmas card,
Some may think that isn't so much.
But, for me it was just wonderful,
It was two years since we'd been in touch.

We'd had a fight some time ago,
I don't even remember the reason.
But, sometimes to get over the hurt,
It often takes more than one season.

I often checked on her through our family,
To make sure she was feeling well,
But, I hesitated to contact her;
On differences, I didn't want to dwell.

So when I received this card today,
It was like a weight had been lifted.
Because for us to have gotten this far,
A lot of "coarse sand" had to be sifted

Now, maybe we can begin again.
As a daughter and a mother.
To forget and forgive all the hurt,
That we have brought upon each other.

A New Year is coming in a few more days,
A great time to make amends.
If we can't be a loving mother and daughter,
At the very least, we can work on being friends.

Just Like a Dance

It's the day after Christmas and my heart is still soaring.
No one could ever tell me this holiday is boring!

I love every moment of it. The shopping to the giving.
I'm so very grateful for this life in which I'm living.

I feel so blessed to once again have had the chance,
To spend time with my children. It's just like a dance.

No matter the melody. It's always so fine.
The rhythm so loving, with these children of mine.

At times it's like a waltz. One, two, three. One, two, three.
Other times, it's more like a sweet flowing symphony.

Then of course, sometimes it's an old fashioned jitterbug.
Or rock and roll. Makes you want to roll up the rug!

Christmas gives us memories of our own special ballet.
But, once again we must put our dancing shoes away.

It's so cheering to know that the melody will play on.
After this Christmas, just as the ones that have gone.

The Sunglasses

She had a close-up taken, with her sunglasses on.
When I asked her why, she said it was to hide.
She said the glasses would cover up the feelings,
So no one could see, what was really inside.

Such beautiful eyes, so deep and so blue,
I could not understand what she said.
But, when she removed her sunglasses,
What I saw filled my heart with dread.

I looked into the eyes of the one I loved,
As I searched for the warmth and the light.
But, instead I found a blankness there,
Something more apt for the night.

What I wanted to see, I was not seeing.
The aura was stark, dark and cold.
I looked into the eyes of my beloved.
I could not perceive her soul.

What happened to this dear loved one?
What took her loving light away?
Was it just too many heartbreaks,
Or the last one, which did finally betray?

I wish I could hold her again in my arms,
To let her know how much she is missed.
This girl with the beautiful deep blue eyes,
That I pray Heavenly angels have kissed.

No Voice

She chose to leave. It was her choice.
She chose to leave. We had no voice.
She took away, a love most dear.
Memories she left are poignantly clear.

She broke our hearts. She'll never know it.
Her heart was broken. She couldn't show it.
She never knew when she was here,
How much she was loved; Was held so dear.

She always cheered us with a note.
Always gave us so much hope.
Always kind, considerate and true.
She said she knew what she had to do.

"Don't worry, Mom. It will be okay.
I don't want you to worry another day."
So kind she was, to say those words.
To ease my heart, trembling like a bird's.

I prayed that night, as never before,
To give her help, ease the pain that she bore.
Early next morning, we got the sad news.
She'd made a decision. Not easy to choose.

We knew then, she wouldn't be back.
Our lives forever altered. One final act.
Life goes on, as we know that it must.
What happened then, to her basic trust?

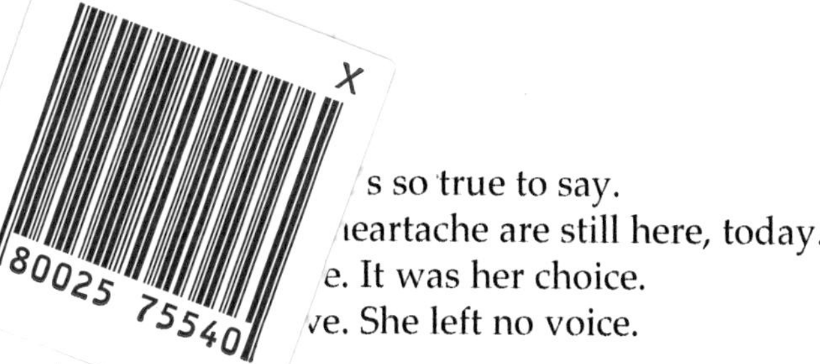

s so true to say.
ieartache are still here, today.
e. It was her choice.
ve. She left no voice.

Note: My ol year old daughter was a teenage mother, and although we never knew it, she had suffered from depression for years. She was under a doctor's care. I was blessed, in that I raised her two children from the time they were 15 and 12. j.

The Mother's Day Message

It was Mother's Day. But, I was feeling so blue.
It would be another day, I wouldn't get a card from you.

I brought out the card you gave me, that last year.
Filled with all the words, a mother wants to hear.

I set it on the table, this card with no date.
Such beautiful words. And not at all late.

My doldrums were mounting, I had to take a walk.
I knew what I needed was to have a little talk.

I came upon a small bench among some leafy trees.
And with a very deep sigh, I fell to my knees.

I asked God why. Was it something I'd done?
Why did she leave? Take away our sun?

I asked Him please, could He give me a sign.
To know she'd found peace, tho' she'd left all behind?

After a long cry, I rose from my knees.
I left the shade of those green leafy trees.

I followed the pathway, all the way home.
I had no desire to wander or roam.

I entered my apartment. Answering machine light blinking.
I pushed the button, without any thinking.

The sweetest voice said, "Mom, just calling to wish you a
Happy Mothers' Day.
You are always in my thoughts. I'm sorry I had to go away."

The message wasn't meant for me. The number was dialed
wrong.
But, the words filled my empty heart, like the words from a
song.

God knew what I needed on this very special day.
When I fell to my knees. When I knelt to pray.

Nothing More To Say

She left this earth sixteen years ago, today.
She left quickly, as if there was nothing more to say.

I miss her laughter, her notes and her calls.
The paintings she had done, still adorn my walls.

I wish I could see her again, and hold her close.
Take away those things that bothered her the most.

A mom can only apply band-aids, or a kiss to a sore spot.
Can only give warnings to not touch a place that's hot.

A mother teaches manners, cleanliness and stories of God.
And then weeps forever, over the body in the sod.

But this is the way it is: Children must live their own lives.
We can only hope to be there, for the high and low dives.

We try to praise, to assure. Of their accomplishments we sing.
Sometimes, it's not enough. Their own bells they need to ring.

Yet, some can't seem to find the peace and the glorious love.
They look all around, but, do they forget to look above?

As a mother, you try to think of what you'd done wrong.
Why she couldn't hear the words in your song.

A mom will carry her guilt, all the days of her life.
Wishing she could have somehow eased her daughter's strife.

But, in essence the truth is, there is nothing she could have done.
Must get on with her own life. Keep looking up to the sun.

So I say prayers today, for the darling girl who went away.
She left so quickly. As if there was nothing more to say.

Those Little Girls

I miss those little girls so much. They don't even know.
It seems like only yesterday. I loved to watch them grow.

I would play with them everyday. Loved to make them laugh.
Used to run with them in the sun. Gave them a bubble bath.

Went for walks down by the tracks. Through the hushed green trees.
We picked wild red strawberries, and watched out for bees

We'd rake the autumn-colored leaves. Great big piles and heaps.
And then we'd run and play and jump. Lovely ballet leaps.

Winter time was cold and snowy. Wonderland of ice.
We'd have cookies and hot chocolate. It wasn't a vice!

Spring wakened with a splendor. The days grew longer.
Through the snow peaked a crocus, as it grew stronger.

We'd read stories and play dress-up, on gray, gloomy days.
Looked for rainbows after a storm. Welcomed the suns rays.

Summer days, we'd spend out on the lawn. Scanning the skies.
Pretending the puffy white clouds, were soft, whipped cream pies.

Memories come back, now and then. When I least expect.
I miss those little girls so much, and how they hugged my neck.

He Is Always There

He always makes sure, that I have enough.
He never leaves me stranded.
He always makes sure, that I have enough,
Though sometimes, it's second handed.

When I'm down and out, don't know what to do,
He brightens my day with ideas.
Before I know it, I'm feeling better,
He has taken away all my fears.

Once, my girls didn't have a coat to wear.
Winter was coming. Snow and cold.
That was the time their grandma sent coats,
Though I'd never the worry told.

When food was scarce, no money to spend,
I found a twenty dollar bill.
We then had enough to see us through.
We tell that story, still.

God has always been there, helping us out,
When all hope was lost.
He's been there to encourage us. Lift us up.
Another river we have crossed.

I could not go on, if it weren't for God's love.
He never leaves me without it.
He always makes sure, that I have enough,
I've never had reason to doubt it.

A Walk In The Park

Some days, you wake up, and you just want to write.
Makes no matter if you, or your house is a fright.
You sit down in front of your computer, and wait.
And then the words come. Like from a flood gate!

You remember friends, who have gone from this light.
Did they accomplish everything that they might?
Everyone has dreams. Some big, and some small.
Did they do all they wanted? Did they risk a fall?

You think of family members. Still on this plane.
Are they having fun? Or do they often complain.
Do they see the sunshine, even on a rainy day?
Do they have faith in God? Do they often pray?

Your children come to mind. The blessing they've been.
The happiness they've brought, to this life that you're in.
Did you teach everything that you should have, for them?
Are they prepared, should their good life turn grim?

Your grandchildren! What an absolute delight!
The time you spend with them. Every day or night,
Comes as a re-run of the life you've been through.
Diapers, birthdays, ballgames. Sometimes the zoo.

As I sit here writing, I remember all the good times.
And sometimes the unsweetened lemons and limes.
But, for what we've been through, we've made our mark,
Life doesn't promise, a walk in the park

Pope John Paul II,

He's been called home, this Holy man,
Who invoked us all to seek God.
He's been called home, this Holy man,
Whose body will now rest in the sod.

He will be sadly missed, this Holy man,
Because of his inspiration.
He will be sadly missed, this Holy man,
Who taught us through his vocation.

He will be glorified, this Holy man,
Who led us all to Jesus' way.
He will be glorified, this Holy man,
He taught us once again to pray.

He will be remembered, this Holy man,
As humbleness he did preach,
He will be remembered, this Holy man,
As by his actions he did teach.

He will be blessed, this Holy man,
God does surely know his name.
He will be blessed, this Holy man,
His love of Jesus, was his fame

His life was a flame, this Holy man,
And he did burn it bright.
His life was a flame, this Holy man,
Into our darkness he brought light.

We will rejoice, for this Holy man,
As he is Heaven bound.
We will rejoice, for this Holy man,
His reward he now has found.

Darling Little Girl

I have a great-grandchild. Of this I'm very proud.
I'd shout it from the roof tops. Mustn't be too loud.

My great-grandchild happens to be a darling little girl,
The first time I saw Hannah, my heart went into a whirl.

When she was fussy, I'd offer to rock her to sleep.
Holding her long after. I'd not make a peep.

To have her snuggle in my arms, is so very sweet,
I could forget to breathe, or at the very least, to eat.

There is nothing in this world that could ever compare,
To holding my dear Hannah. Smelling her hair.

I know that I'm older now and have seen a lot in this world,
But, I still look forward to tomorrow, and being with that little
girl.

How fortunate I am to have been blessed with her in my life,
Makes me forget completely that there was ever any strife.

I have a great-grandchild, of this I'm very proud.
What the heck. I'm just going to shout it out loud!

Being A Kid Again

Went to bed last night feeling so young and carefree,
But, then this morning I awoke.
Being a kid again, hit me hard from head to toe,
And that, regretfully, is no joke.

Nothing beats playing with a five year old grandchild,
My imagination, unstifled, soars.
But, with this mornings burst of sunlight in my eyes,
I think I should just stay indoors.

I ache from the top of my head, to the bottom of my feet,
Yet, remember the joy that I felt.
As we swam and dove into the deep blue pool, blissfully
Unaware of the punishment dealt.

But, now as I sit here, my aching muscles a tribute,
To youth too soon gone,
I see the folly of my ways, as I search for an aspirin,
To relieve the basis of my moan.

Knowing full well, that we'll be right back at it,
As sure as the day is long.
Because that feeling of being a kid again, shouldn't
Be wasted on the young.

Grandma's Lament

I remember the times we set bugs free,
When they wandered where they shouldn't.

The poor frogs that were run over in the roads,
When they tried to hop away, but couldn't.

The tickle times, and the bubble baths.
Making instant coffee, scrambling eggs.

Toasted waffles, floating in warm syrup.
And how you worried about your skinny legs.

We played hide and seek. Your house or mine.
I read to you a lot and rocked you, too.

Told you stories of when you were a baby,
When all you could say was, "Ga-ga" and "Goo."

We painted pictures and attempted to sew.
And watched cartoons while we ate.

The afternoons we practiced drawing numbers,
And especially the number eight.

Now you're off to Kindergarten. All grown up.
I'll wait patiently at home.

Recalling some of the things we did,
And writing this silly poem.

The Clear Blue Sky

Out of the clear blue sky,
My five year old Great-granddaughter did say,
"Grandma, I worry all the time,
That I will forget you someday."

I smiled as I reminded her of how often
We had learned new games together.
How we would swim in the pool, and
Have picnics on the floor, in bad weather.

The times we painted pictures, and tried to sew.
And watched cartoons while we ate.
The hours we spent learning to draw numbers,
Especially the number eight.

The times we had talks of God and Life.
And discussed being good or bad…and things.
We talked of telling fibs, and hurting others.
And when we do good deeds, Angels get their wings.

She asked, "Who's God's Mother, or did He make Himself?
Is God everywhere? And if so, how could that be?"
I had to tell her sometimes, I didn't know the answer,
But, when I've called out to Him, He has answered me.

Then I told her, "There is no way you could forget me.
Nor is there anything that could make me forget you.
I will always feel that I am as close as your skin,
And as deep as your heart, because our love is so true."

I Crossed My Fingers

What can I tell this little girl who is almost five?
When she asks me how much longer I will be alive.

It's on her mind every time we see each other.
It's hard because I'm her great-grandmother.

What can I say that will ease her worried mind?
I see how she looks at my face, which is lined.

If I complain even a little about an ache or a pain,
Her expression seems to say, "Oh, no. Not again!"

Then she implores me not to go to Heaven without her.
She looks deep into my eyes. I have no reason to doubt her.

She's not even five years old! Has a lifetime before her.
I tell her I will leave her someday. That I'll always adore her.

But, she wants me to promise that to Heaven I won't go.
So I cross my fingers and lie to her. Because I do love her so.

And then I pray each night that God will let me stay one more day.
While I try to think of words, which will take her fears away.

What can I tell this little girl who is not yet five?
When she asks me how much longer I will be alive.

Champions Just Can't Help It!

I had the most profound experience the other day,
As my granddaughter and I played a game.
She is only five years old, but, was trouncing me!
I, of course, praised her on this bit of fame.

This little girl and I are pals, as if we're the same age.
She often encourages me. Hates to see me lose!
(Probably because I'm so dramatic about it.)
But, I know full well, I have to pay my dues.

On and on we go, playing until late afternoon.
She keeps amassing cards, and piling them up high.
While I truly do my best, to add to my hoard.
She looks at me with patience. Gives a soft sigh.

She then started "helping" me to improve my score.
She'd give me little hints, and motion to a card.
I really didn't want her to help me. It wouldn't be fair!
But to beat her honestly, was really getting hard.

I decided that I should tell her, that cheating isn't right.
Even if she was doing it to make me feel better.
We should always do our very best, in everything we do.
Meaning we should follow rules to the letter!

She seemed to understand, as we continued the game.
But, scored again, although I had dealt it!
Then she looked at me with those big brown eyes, and said,
"I'm sorry, Grandma. Champions just can't help it!"

Little Gimpy

My five year old granddaughter and I
Walk quietly each day, to the pond.
Ducks float serenely together.
Among them, there seems to be a bond.

Mostly white ducks, a few grays and browns.
One looks like a very small mallard.
We notice that he can hardly walk,
Yet, maintains an air of stalwart.

Little Gimpy, the name we gave him,
Cheerfully wags his little tail.
Each day we lovingly bring him bread,
His color now beginning to pale.

We fed him, away from the others,
To be sure he received a fair share.
But, then one day he did not get up.
My granddaughter and I knelt in pray'r

"He's not here anymore, is he, Gram?,"
She hesitatingly asked of me.
I told her he'd gone to Duck Heaven.
Where now he could run. He was free!

Little Gimpy taught us a lesson.
He showed us how to live every day:
Be cheerful, no matter our problems.
Show our gratitude in every way.

Giving Thanks

We're all getting together in Florida this year,
To celebrate Thanksgiving, and share our good cheer.

We're so glad to be here. We've been too long apart.
Although, quite honestly, we're always together in heart.

We've a lot to be thankful for, once again.
As we sit down to eat, with family and friend.

Our teenagers are really doing quite well in school,
And in sports they've proven they are "real cool."

Our kindergarten student is also doing very well,
She knows her numbers and ABC's. Great stories she can tell.

We grownups in our chosen fields are also doing fine,
We wish only, that we could give our families a little more time.

This year we welcome new people to our circle of love.
We know that those who have left us, look on from above.

We'll have a big turkey, with many a trimming.
The platters, and bowls are all filled and brimming.

We will not complain, to any great degree,
For the fruits of our labors are very plain to see.

We'll simply thank God for our good fortune and health,
Asking that He'll give us wisdom, along with our wealth.

We'll thank Him also, for keeping us safe through this year,
When storms ravaged our area, and actually came quite near.

The elections are at last over, and we're thankful for it,
And we pray, that in the White House the best man does sit.

We ask God to watch over our warriors around this great earth,
And pray that they know, that we're aware of their worth.

So Dear God, as we gather to thank you on this special holiday,
Please listen to our words, as together, we bow our heads to pray.

The Sunshine of Their Lives

I find myself drawn to this keyboard again today.
I don't have any idea of what I'm going to say.

I can always write about my grandchildren. Any time.
It's really quite easy to think of a jingle or a rhyme.

To my being they bring so much pleasure and joy,
They make this keyboard seem like it's my toy.

I can write of their accomplishments, at this young age.
I see their lives unfold. A book opened to each page.

They learn to walk. Then suddenly they are talking.
Then it's Pre-k, dancing classes. Then T-Balls, they're stalking.

Snapshots of homeruns, swimming and other triumphs galore.
And as much as I'm included, I still want more.

I want to actually be there, for each hurdle they overcome.
I want to hug and comfort them, when they happen to miss some.

I want to let them know, it's okay to sometimes lose a race.
That although winning is wonderful, losing teaches us grace.

I want to be around them as they blossom into their teens.
See the change in them, as they go from diapers to jeans

Too quickly they are having sleepovers, trying makeup,
babysitting.
Going to camp, then proms. Suddenly tuxedos they're fitting.

Then they're off to college. They are ready. A great future in
their plans.
And I regret that time flows so quickly, through the hour glass
of sands.

So I go back through those snapshots. The little notes of cheer.
I bask in the sunshine of their lives. Brush away my selfish
tear.

I pray they will be happy and their dreams they will surpass.
I thank God that I can see their future. Have been part of their
past

We Need To Protect Them

I never met Jessica. Never knew her at all.
Yet her face is forever etched into my mind.
I see her innocence. Her purity. Her smile
The gentleness she showed to mankind.

We cry because we realize her terror.
We realize just what this world has lost.
We cry because Jessica paid the ultimate price.
It was just too great a cost.

What can we do to improve their world?
To make it safe for our little girls and boys.
We need to have laws to protect them.
So we can better shelter our greatest joys.

Though I never met Jessica. She is our wake-up call.
We must rapidly change this world around.
Protect the little children with all our strength.
So happiness can be theirs…and abound.

After the darkness always comes the light.
Of this fact, we have complete trust.
Jessica is home, where she belongs.
We will go on, as we must.

We will never forget this sweet Jessie.
She will live forever in our heart.
The memory of her will jump out at us all,
God will comfort us. We're never far apart.

I never met Jessica. Never knew her at all.
Yet her face is forever etched into my heart.
I feel her innocence. Her purity. Her smile.
Telling us to hug our children, each time we part.

Happy Birthday to My Daughter

Since everything I write, seems to end up in rhyme,
I thought I'd give it a try, at least one more time.

I don't even have to think of something to rhyme with Eileen.
What makes it so simple, is that you were crowned Queen.

And now it's your birthday, I won't mention which one,
But, I don't see how it can be, when I'm only forty-one!

So I'll just wish you the best in this silly sort of way,
And thank you for being born, on that particular day.

I thank you for the blessing you have always been,
The sparkle in your Irish eyes, that wonderful grin.

The way a phone call can please me, with your cheery, "Hi
Mom"
When I'm upset with something, you make me feel so calm.

Your hugs, so gentle, so strong, so tight. All in one minute.
Make me glad for my life, and for having you in it.

We've shared many glad times, some scary, some sad.
We've helped each other, through the good and the bad.

Memories of you, make me laugh, make me cry.
And I hate it each time, we need to say goodbye.

I celebrate this day, because to me you were born,
On that lovely Sunday, at seven in the morn.

Happy Birthday, Dear Eileen. I know it's your day.
But, you were my gift, my very own sunray.

Keep that smile on your face and God in your heart.
Have fun. Be careful. Always be smart.

Note: Eileen was the first girl born during "National Business
Women's Week."
Hence the queen designation. j.

My First Granddaughter

I remember that wonderful day when you were born.
We'd gone to the hospital, early that morn.

Thirty-one hours went by. She had labored all through it.
Finally, you were born. We knew she could do it!

What a beautiful little girl, dark hair, skin so rosy.
Snuggled in your pink blanket, all warm and cozy.

What a delight you have been, to all who have loved you.
So quick with a smile, and a big hug, too.

You warm our hearts, with the kind words you say.
You've made some very sad times, turn out okay.

You're intelligent, pretty, have a gorgeous figure.
But, never put on airs. Never try to act "bigger."

Just a sweet, considerate, kind human being.
You make us believe in you; the girl that we're seeing.

Thank you for all you do for our family tree.
And especially for all that you've done for me.

You were my first grandchild, Sweet Aubri Lynn.
I am so happy, that it's my life you are in.

I don't have to tell you of the sorrow, at one time I felt.
Nor how I thought the ice around my heart, would never melt.

And you could never guess the lovely pleasure you bring.
It's because of you, that my heart learned again to sing.

Have a wonderful day. Be happy! Laugh a Lot!
If I could, I would give you a really big yacht.

I will always wish you happiness, good health and love.
And pray that God will forever bless you, from above.

My Delight

Happy birthday to Alan, my first-born grandson.
You've been such a delight to me, from day one!

You always were so cute, in an impish sort of way.
Though sometime I thought I'd be prematurely gray!

But, you were quite loving. And grew up just fine.
I loved your sense of humor. You had quite a line.

You brought me a lot of joy, when the days were so sad.
And I tried not to act too angry, when you made me mad.

Most of the time, I was proud of you. I was your biggest fan.
Even when you got into trouble, you faced it like a man.

We've come a long way together, in this crazy sort of life.
You've helped heal my heart. Helped to ease the strife.

I love you more than you could ever begin to guess.
I will always wish for you, whatever makes you happiest.

Thank you for coming into my life. You've made it so great.
Happy birthday, dear Alan. In my heart, you're first rate!

Edward the Fourth

Edward the Fourth, what a wonderful name.
Does it ever make you think, that you might have fame?

Names are important. (At least you know who to blame).
But, you have to think about it. Your name is the same.

Do you ever think of those who came before you?
And wonder what it was, that they did or didn't do?

Did Edward the First know at the time that he was?
And did he question it, or just accept it, because.

And what of the others? Did they know their role?
Or did they decide to just go with the roll?

Well, I know you're special. You're my dear grandson.
You're intelligent, kind and really quite handsome.

I love your phone calls, that keep me up to date,
On all the great things, you've done as of late.

Your baseball games, campout trips, and blue karate belt.
And when you call me "Grammy." It makes my heart melt.

You have character, and character really counts.
It's what helps when all else fails. It gives us that bounce!

It's what keeps us going. And at the end of the day,
We can say we did our best. Then just put it away.

I'm so glad you share your life with me, when you can
I can picture in my mind, how you'll be as a man.

So, Edward the Fourth, Happy Birthday to you.
You make me so proud, of all the things that you do.

Have fun on your birthday. Celebrate! Be loud!
I wish I could be with you, as part of the crowd.

God Bless you, Dear Edward, in all that you do.
I will always pray, that all your wishes come true.

A Love Note to Morgan

A love note to granddaughter, Morgan. You are so dear.
What would my life have been like, if you hadn't been here?

You've brought so many sunny days to this life of mine.
Have made me so very proud, that you're a part of my vine.

We used to go exploring when you were only two.
Saw real and imaginary animals, more apt for the zoo.

We'd go to the mall and play hide and seek,
As around the pillars we'd hide and then peek.

Bubble baths were one of your favorite things.
We'd make sudsy butterflies and angels with wings.

You'd often crawl in bed with me. Sheets over our heads,
As we made up stories, about the design on the spreads.

We used to hold hands as we ran errands to the store.
Sadly, I knew the day would come. We wouldn't do that
anymore.

Yet, you've made all your visits so very special to me.
I've seen you grow. I can see the woman you will be.

So keep your eyes focused on the future that lies ahead.
You'll have nothing to fear. Nothing to dread.

You are a strong person. This trait will see you through.
Plus your great looks, personality and brains, too!

I love you, dear Morgan. I have from the start.
You came into this world, and dove straight into my heart.

Bitter-Sweet Day

The first day that I saw you, my sweet Cassondra Ann,
Was in the Palm Beach Airport right after the plane did land.

When your mom handed you to me, it was a great surprise.
Such a darling baby girl. Made tears come to my eyes.

Your parents had come to visit, but, it was not a happy day.
You see, your dad's sister (my daughter) had just passed away.

They had brought you along to cheer me, of that I'm very sure.
Their intentions were so kind and loving. So very pure.

I held you close to my heart that day, and as my tear drops fell,
I whispered a "thank you" to God, and prayed that all would be
well.

Time has gone by since that bitter-sweet day. My heart will
never heal.
But, knowing you, and having you in my life, has helped a great
deal.

Your sweet "Hi Grandma Zee," when part of your life you
share,
Makes me feel so warm and special, just to know that you care.

I love to hear of your latest achievements, and get pictures in
the mail,
When I see your lovely face and beautiful smile, it just makes
my heart sail.

Each night, as I get ready for bed, I pray for your safety,
happiness and health.
I also pray that you will have wisdom. It's worth even more
than wealth.

The words "sweet sixteen" seem to fit you like a very soft
glove.
I wish I could celebrate with you, but you know I send my
love.

You've been a special grandchild to me, all your lifetime
through,
I wish you the very best birthday, and wish you fun in all you
do.

So Happy Birthday, my Sweet Cassondra, have a wonderful
day!
That all your dreams come true, is what I'll always pray.

Anniversary Wishes

Happy anniversary! What a wonderful time to reflect
On where you were and how far you've come.
Look all around you. See your accomplishments.!
Your children, your careers, your home.

The memories you've made in all your travels.
The people you've met along the way.
The love and respect you have for each other,
The way you've kept God, in your every day.

The citizenship you teach, just by being involved.
Yet retaining the part that makes you unique.
The time and love you give to your children,
As into their future, you get a little peek.

And through all of this, you take care of each other.
You listen and advise, share the work load.
You have learned to understand the other's needs.
You have helped each other, stay on the right road.

Love is the answer to any questions you may have.
Letting the other know, on you they can depend.
Knowing when to bite your tongue, and when
To speak up, but only doing so, as a friend.

You've come a long way since you began
This journey of sharing your days.
And you've been blessed, as you well know,
In the most wonderful, happiest way.

Misunderstandings

Misunderstandings. How complex our lives have become.
When only complaints, instead of thanks, are the sum.
The time we spend, regretting the days gone by.
And yet in a moment, it seems we didn't really try.

Why don't we try to walk in another's shoes? Do they pinch?
Why can't we see the other's side? Give at least an inch.
How is it that an "I'm sorry," comes with a lowly, " but."
And an "It's all right," is delivered at times with a cut.

What is wrong with this world? Why always a duel?
When all we need to do, is follow the Golden Rule.
To treat each other as we would like to be treated.
And when a wrong is done. Don't remain seated.

Stand up. Speak out. Make our intentions clear.
We know we've offended. Remove the flames that sear.
Life is too short. We must quickly atone.
Life is a gift, we all believe. But, in fact, it's a loan.

We are here such a short time. Why waste it on hurts.?
Why say things in anger? Nasty remarks in spurts.
We must realize that what we say are mere rantings.
Can have lasting affects. Make for poor understandings.

Misunderstandings Our lives are so complex.
Complaints instead of thanks. Wrong reflects.
Wasting precious time regretting things that were said.
We can never change the outcome, once we are dead.

Enough Time

I just received the news that my aunt had passed away.
She had been a very good person right up to the day.

They say that she had carried her bills to the mailbox,
Then returned to her chair, her television to watch.

Death came at that moment, to take her on her way.
Gave her the time she needed, for her bills to pay.

It makes you wonder if we will all have enough time,
To get everything finished. It would be so sublime.

To have time to say goodbye. To give that final hug.
To think back to when we were young and felt so snug.

To have time to thank those who at your side, stood by.
Were there when you laughed. Heard your sad cry.

Picked you up, when to the side you were falling.
Were always there, at your beck and calling.

To have time to tell your children of the great joy,
Of having known them. Each girl and each boy.

Having time to tell your siblings, they meant so much.
That life was made better, by their soft touch.

Time to reflect on what had been accomplished. Or not.
One last moment for a prayer, or a note to jot.

We shouldn't waste time on what could have been.
Instead, make each day count. It's golden, not tin.

We don't know when our last day will be here.
Better to just live each one. Without any fear.

If we do the best we can, each day on this earth,
God will know that we are thankful, that he gave us birth.

Counting Sheep

This is one of those mornings when I just need to write.
I went to bed, to get some sleep, but was up all night!
It's so strange the way it happens, my brain will not sleep.
I toss and I turn, and then of course I count those sheep.

Which is a silly thing to do, when you think of it.
Why sheep? Why not cows? Or whatever else that may fit.
But, I just lay there, tired out and in a daze.
Knowing that soon the sun will be spreading its rays.

Thoughts keep going through my sleepless mind, of the news
The bombings, the kidnappings. People singing the blues.
I wish I could do something to ease the pains of the day.
But, the only thing I know, is to kneel and to pray.

I get out of bed for the umpteenth time, and hoping the last.
As I kneel down, I firmly fold my hands in a tight grasp.
Asking our Dear Father in Heaven, to help us with our pains.
Teach us when we use our hearts, we must also use our brains.

Such a simple concept. Humans have the gift of reason.
We should be able to contend, no matter the season.
We should be able to figure a way to live, agreeably.
So that our grandchildren can have a future, foreseeably.

A new day is now here. I made it through the night.
The only bad thing is, all day I'll look a fright!
The main thing I've learned, now that I'm up and dressing.
Ensure a good night's sleep, by counting each blessing.

God is always listening. He's up all night, too.
He pays attention to our thoughts and what we do.
And once again, I've learned that prayers are a must.
He gave us our hearts and brains. In God we must trust.

The Mask

It's Halloween. One of my favorite times of the year.
I love to wear a mask. But none that one would fear.

I've been a good witch, a fortune teller, and even a clown.
And it's a lot of fun to dress up in an evening gown.

To be someone else; to put on another's face,
Allows me to be free. At least in that time. At that place.

I walk a little differently. My voice is a little bit loud.
It feels great for the moment, to stand out, in a crowd.

But, soon the party is over. I take off the mask and go home.
I start planning for next year. Deciding who I will become.

God Always Has A Plan

God never turns His back on us,
He has a plan, this we must trust.
Tho' days and nights may pass in pain,
He will be with us, and we will gain.

We need to believe with all our heart,
He promises us a brand new start.
Some doors close. It is as they must.
We then prepare, as forward we're thrust.

God knows we really don't want to go.
We were happy with the status quo.
But, it's His plan that we must obey.
He's so excited to show us the way.

God's plans are always the very best.
We never have need to second guess.
Just open our minds and hearts today,
Give Him ourselves to do as He may.

Once we do this, with no reservation,
Things will happen. No imagination.
I speak from experience when I say,
God wants our confidence, this very day.

So before we go to bed each night,
Let Him know that we know He is right.
That we'll look forward to His plan.
That we believe and we understand.

Doors will be opened. Dreams will come true.
We'll not be downhearted or even blue.
So look forward with a smile on our face.
God has a plan and we are in His Grace.

The Fourth of July

The Fourth of July! I hear those words
And memories leap into my mind.
Of years gone by, in what seems now,
To have been a much easier time.

We'd get up early on that special day,
Go to the parade, with our red, white and blue.
See the marching bands from the Elks, The Moose Club,
And of course our own high school.

Everyone so happy. Pointing here and there!
Little children gleefully jumping up and down.
Parents trying to calm them a little bit,
As candy rained down from a clown.

The odor of fireworks, mixed with other scents
Of Hot Dogs, Hamburgers and Cotton Candy.
Young ladies all dressed up in their finery,
Young men were dressed up too. Looking quite dandy.

We seemed happier then, more apt to give a smile.
We put our worries aside for the day.
Happy to show pride for our great country.
And in plain view, we'd bow our heads and pray.

I wish my children could see how it was back then.
When people more patriotic seemed.
When pride of country was shared by everyone.
When many could relate to "I Have A Dream."

I'm very thankful that I lived when I did.
I know times change as they are destined to do.
And when I hear the sounds of the Fourth of July,
My heart still sings for the Red, White and the Blue.

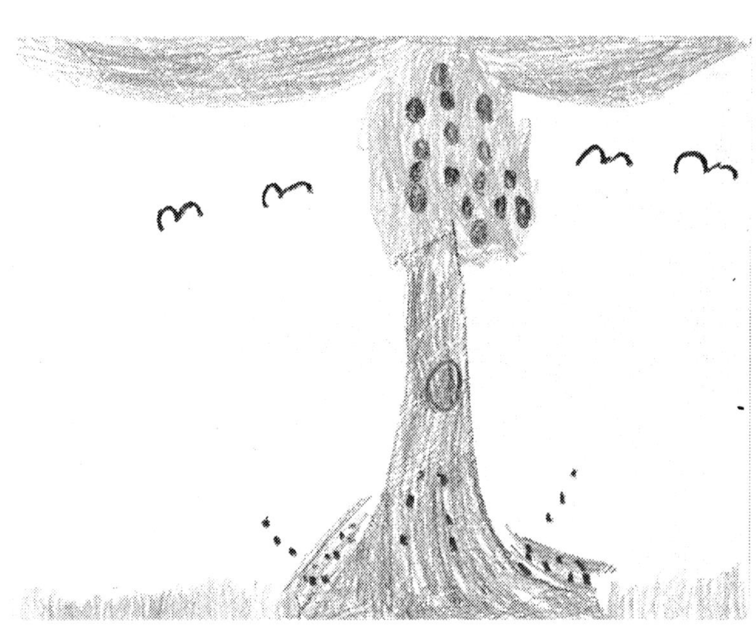

The Scavengers

Have you ever seen those big, black, scavenger birds?
Those that are usually found around a dump site.
I saw them just today. Fourteen to be exact.
They were gathered on top of the roof, in plain sight.

I don't know what to think, but I doubt this is good.
Reminds me of Edgar Allen Poe's "The Raven."
It's evil, and scary and terribly eerie.
I thought desperately of finding a safe haven.

After quite a long while, the birds left that high roof.
It seemed to be a majority decision.
They flew away as if in a unit of one.
Those eerie birds flew high, in perfect precision.

Now they're swooping down, playing 'Follow the Leader'.
But, it's not in a jovial, lighthearted way.
They peer and they probe with their beady little eyes.
Looking for creatures that might soon become their pray.

After many hours, their game became boring.
At least that is the impression that seemed to be.
They flew off toward a faraway horizon,
Leaving a frightened and very unsettled me.

Why am I having these feelings of an omen?
What sort of wicked 'sign' could this be portending?
Do I just look away, and hope that we'll be safe?
Instead of evil, expect a happy ending?

Well, I'll try, because it's my nature to do so.
After all, they did go away. Isn't that right?
That should give a not very sinister meaning.
But, to feel safer. I'll pray extra hard tonight.

People of Freedom

The terrorists have performed another beheading.
They say it is for Allah. That they do his bidding.
How can an Allah who they say advocates peace,
Uphold these butcherings, more apt for the Beast?

How can these terrorists even begin to think,
That people will be swayed by the depths that they sink?
We aren't afraid. We're of a much stronger ilk.
Our mantle is bravery. Not gold, burlap or silk.

We are people of freedom. Well aware of the price.
We will not back down. Will not try to be nice.
Our hearts break for the families so sorely tested.
And at the same time look with pride at the value invested.

We believe in a God who gives love. Without restriction.
It's a very simple concept. No contradiction.
Our lives we value greatly, while here on this earth.
We must try to give value to our life. That's the worth.

The means of our deaths, sometimes shocking, always sad.
Can not take away the shared memories, we had.
God does not cause these acts of violence to take place.
He will help us through the heartache, with his loving Grace.

He preaches do unto others, as you would have them do.
He gives us the knowledge, to think it through.
Our freedoms we value. We'll protect them to all ends.
We've done it before. Some enemies are now our friends.

Not many of us have riches, or houses of gold.
What we do own, not tangible. Not quite so bold.
We own the right to an education, to work. Have unhampered trips.
To enjoy our country and our lives on this land, or on ships.

To enjoy our children. Encourage them in our ways.
Be happy in their growth. Allow them to enjoy their days.
We have the choice of religion, (or sadly) none.
We aren't dictated to, by anyone.

We will continue to help the oppressed and the poor.
It's our "thank you" for the way of life, we adore.
So as we mourn another beheading of an innocent man.
We know in our hearts that God always has a plan.

We'll pray for his family and friends, to lessen their strife.
To give the utmost honor to this man and his life.
He was there to help the people, as well as earn a living.
It makes no sense at all to have killed him. He was so giving.

We must stand up to these murderers. Can't let them just walk away.
This man must not have died in vain. Their debt they must pay.
We don't know all the answers, but we do know what is right.
We must stay very strong. In our minds, in our hearts and in our might.

He Threatened Us Again

Osama bin Laden has again raised his ugly head.
He wants to instill in America, a feeling of dread.
He just doesn't understand our wonderful way of life.
Thinks he can destroy us by threatening war and strife.

Of course we would like to live as we have in the past.
But, over this life, he has tried to throw a dark cast.
He thinks it's wrong to be loving and kind, and always willing
to share.
Simply cannot fathom our feelings. Doesn't know how much
we care.

He cannot understand our freedom and how much we do
adore it.
He doesn't understand, either, that we will fight ferociously
for it.
We fought for our basic freedoms, over two-hundred years
ago.
We've fought several times since then. That struggle we well
know.

We've worked hard to build this nation. It took blood, sweat
and tears.
Through it all we've learned, no one will ever control us with
fears.
We have welcomed people from other nations, all around this
world.
They've pledge allegiance to our beautiful flag, whenever it's
unfurled.

And still they come, of their own free accord, to more fully
enrich their lives.
Working hard in our cities, in factories and on farms.
Husbands and wives.
Their children go to better schools. Have many opportunities
to advance.
These people keep coming here for a better life. They want to
take the chance.

Our country is a mosaic. Our lands, our rivers and our fields.
Our people are a mosaic, also. They'll never give up their
ideals.
So Osama, don't you dare come near us with your evil, Satanic
ways.
Stay in your mountains with the inhabitants who wear masks,
and hide in caves.

We may not always be perfect. But, we strive for brotherly
love.
Our strength over our enemies has always come from above.
Our God is loving. He teaches the Golden Rule and to turn the
other cheek.
But, He's also taught us to beware of Satan. And asks that we
not be weak.

Osama, don't darken our doors with your bullish threats.
For our liberty, we'll always fight.
You've awakened the peacefully sleeping giant.
We are united. You'll feel our might.

The Sacred Prize

The terrorists struck in London today.
People injured, killed. Complete dismay.

Innocent ones, with no evil in mind,
Succumbed to terror of the very worst kind.

People in a daze, walking the street.
Lives shattered. Feelings of defeat.

What is going on in this world of ours?
To rain down this terror. Horrific showers.

The height of rush hour. People going to work.
This evil demon chooses to wait and to lurk.

Blameless citizens. Trying to make a living.
Kiss their loved ones goodbye. So giving.

Then as they travel to their destinations,
Attacks come from many diverse locations.

No place to run. Nowhere to hide.
The bombs meant to serve only to deride.

To make people feel afraid. Incomplete.
So the terrorists can more easily, try for defeat.

But, these good people will not give in.
They will stand-up, again and again.

What the terrorists, don't seem to realize;
Freedom from tyranny is a sacred prize.

The attacked ones will ever protect their ways,
They will rise once again from these evil ways.

Freedom is worth every ounce of sacrifice.
It separates good men, from the evil of vice.

Hometown Boy

I never met your son. And yet my heart aches and I too, grieve.
He was the little boy at the park, who once there, never wanted to leave.

He's the little boy who brought home his works of art from school.
That covered your refrigerator. He thought that was so cool!

He's the little boy you cuddled when he fell and scraped his knee.
The same little boy who tried many times, to climb that big old tree.

He grew up, went off to high school, and made you so very proud.
He was a good person, got great marks, stood out in a crowd.

His quick wit, his sense of humor, brought a smile to your face.
And all the while, you admired his style and good grace.

He was of a kind and gentle nature. His Lord he did love.
He answered to this higher power, which comes from above.

He was a faithful servant, and knew God would show him the way.
He made the decision to join the service. Many hours he did pray.

He joined the Marine Corps, to help advance his hopes and dreams.
To go into law enforcement, was just one of his wonderful schemes.

He went off to Iraq, this little boy, who too soon became a man.
He helped his fellow soldiers. Was always quick to give a hand.

Then God called him home. It's sometimes hard to know the reason.
But, we try to accept what we cannot change. We know there is a season.

A time to sow A time to reap. A time to live and a time to die.
He is where he is meant to be. He would be sad to hear you cry.

God understands your grief. He too, gave his much loved son.
And in your heart of hearts, you know—God's Will Be Done.

Remember the things that made you smile and laugh, way back when.
And know that it is God's great plan...that you will meet again.

Did We Make Someone Cry?

Do you ever wish that you could make a difference in these times of strife?
Ever wonder what it is that you're supposed to accomplish in your own life?

We arise each morning. Go about our sometimes commonplace chores.
And then at the end of the day, we simply close our windows and doors.

What did we do in the meantime, as the hours ticked unwaveringly by?
Did we say "hello" to our neighbors? Or did we make someone cry?

I don't think we always realize the impressions we make on another.
We sometimes may be hurtful. Other times, we tend only to smother.

I think the best things we can do, in these most uncertain days.
Is to teach others by example. And give them honest praise.

To try to look at others without a preconceived notion.
To see the good in them and consider their devotion.

Think of the person in your life who most influenced you. Good or bad.
And decide how to make that power work for you. To make you glad.

I feel that our lives are planned for us. But, we have the freedom of will.
And for each day we spend on this earth, we will be presented a bill.

So we must try to be the person we would want someone else to be.
And with this modest insight, our conclusion will set us free.

To Ease Another's Woe

There are so many things I want to say,
To ease another's woe.
To instill that friends are always there.
Where ever we may go.

To always look for the sunshine,
Especially on a stormy day.
That God gave us bright rainbows
To brighten clouds of gray.

That silver linings have been seen
Up in the turbulent skies.
To remind each of us of the love,
To us, He never denies.

Keep memories of the good times,
In every deed and thought.
God knows before we even know,
The blessings we have sought

Thoughts and prayers are with you now,
As you in this illness lay.
Your friends and family wish you well,
Each moment of every day.

God feels our pain and knows our prayers,
In every day or night.
He will not leave in our bleakest hour,
We're always in His sight.

A Prayer of Hope

Word has come to us, of a friend's illness.
We are asked to pray.
To help our dear friend overcome this affliction,
As in bed she lay.

Together, as one, we will make our prayers heard.
To help uplift her hopes.
Letting her know that along with prayers for health,
We pray that she copes.

Ailments at any time, are not what we'd wish for.
Help her to be strong.
Let her know that her friends are steadfast in their thoughts.
Let's urge her along.

We pray that her illness does abate, and that soon
She'll be on the mend.
Writing again, the poems that we love to read.
Ones she loves to pen.

Let her know that she is loved and is missed by all.
We wish her Godspeed.
That to have her back in our group of like minds, is
Our prayer indeed!

I'm the Same One

When I made the decision to move away,
I honestly thought it was so I could start a new day.

A new life sounded so exciting to me...and free.
I thought at last I could do as I pleased, and be me.

But, the me I turned out to be, is the same as before.
And I'm relieved to say, I found in me, a good core.

I've been able to know me better, while out on my own,
Learned to be more moderate. Learned to condone.

Sometimes, to get a better look, it's good to step away.
Like when you admire an oil painting, in the light of day.

Things just look different. The blacks are more gray.
Perspectives change. You learn there's more than one way.

Don't worry about breaking. It's much easier to bend.
Learn to use your new voice, as your ear you do lend.

Be the friend to others that you'd like them to be to you.
Give them room to grow, to find their own way, too.

You discover that life is too short, to spend it in the past.
It's important that you live each day, as though it's your last.

I remember my mother saying, there is no tomorrow.
This thought in my young mind, was full of sorrow.

But, now I see what it was, that my mother meant.
If you live in the moment, it is time well spent.

So don't try to run away from the you that is you,
It matters not where you are, it only matters what you do.

A Happily "Singled" Woman

So many things on my mind, I don't know where to start.
I sit at this keyboard, and find that I want to pour out my heart.

And yet, I feel inhibited, as if I my words, I should mince.
But, then I think, "what the heck!" There shouldn't be any hints.

I live alone, and I'm not unhappy. This seems to bother some.
I don't know why. It's not as though I have anything to run from.

I love to be able to get up at four o'clock in the morning,
And not have to make excuses, nor in fact, give any warning.

If I want to stay up all night, and sleep late the next day,
There's no one to say if it is, or if it isn't okay.

By living alone, it's not always necessary to be saying I'm sorry.
Just do what I want, and when I want. Don't even have to hurry.

Why are there always trade-offs? Why can't we just be?
Why is it, when we do for ourselves, we feel guilty?

I love the freedom of coming and going as I please.
But, sometimes, I miss the "God Bless You," when I sneeze.

A Trusted Friend

Isn't it just great to have a friend you can trust?
One that would visit your home, and never look for dust.

One that when she plans a party, you're at the top of her list.
And when you get some sad news, her eyes mist.

When you're too fat for your clothes, and ask her to go shopping,
She's not unkind, when she sees your buttons are popping.

She never nitpicks, is snobby, or makes a snide remark.
And she really listens, even when you talk until dark.

She doesn't repeat stories, you tell her in confidence.
And she doesn't gossip about you, over the back fence.

And when you haven't seen her, as is the case of late.
When you do meet, the first thing she says is, "You look great!."

She makes no mention that you're getting old.
She treats you as though you were made of gold.

A friend such as this, I have been truly blessed to know.
I'll never take her friendship for granted. I do love her so.

I'm so comfortable with her. In anything we do.
She's fun. Not demanding. Just tried and true.

She's like a sister to me. Someone I feel I have known,
From a long time ago. Before I called this earth home.

I hope that I am the friend to her, that she is to me.
She makes me a better person, than I ever thought I could be.

Departed Friends

Poems are rattling around in my mind.
I don't know why, and don't know what kind.

The words seem to come from somewhere inside,
I feel like I'm part of a very fast ride.

I find myself thinking of friends who've departed.
And yet, think of myself as just getting started!

I miss the old times, the happy and the sad.
I remember the laughs and the tears that we had.

We shared them all, cloudy days or sunny.
We were very poor, but only lacked money.

Running through the raindrops, on a stormy day.
Skipping in the sunshine. Always ready to play!

Shared clothing, shared books. Homework done together.
Thoughts of red colored gloves, made of rich leather.

Secrets were told, shared stories of dreams.
We were going places. So many schemes!

Friends have departed. But, sweet memories remain.
Maybe someday, we'll be together again.

Just Wondering...

It seems the older I get, the more I wonder about things.
For instance, I wonder why it is, that I wasn't born with wings.

If I had been, I could have traveled the world over.
To the outback in Australia, or maybe the White Cliffs of Dover.

I wonder what it would have been like to have lived so long ago.
To have been in the land of pyramids, or to have met a Pharaoh.

And I wonder why our Ears weren't named Hears, since
That is what we do with them.
Why were our Eyes, not designated as Sees,
It would not have made them more dim.
Did you ever think about Feet, and why
We don't call them Walks?
And of course there are our Mouths,
Which could have easily been called Talks.

I guess I could go on and on with this line of wondering,
But, I won't, because, I do know one thing:

God made each of us, the way He thought we should be
I'm not really questioning the way He made me.

But, as strange as the names for our bodily parts may be,
He gave us each a Heart, and all of these things, for free.

Note: I wrote this one day with 5 year old Hannah, when we were being just a little bit silly. j.

Glad Tidings

I've had a lot of birthdays. I don't need to be precise!
Some of the ones I remember, weren't all that nice.

But, the ones I prefer to think about, now that I am older,
Are the ones that fill my heart, and a very thick folder!

The notes and letters and cards, with cheery sentiments.
The gifts of flowers, scarves and lovely smelling scents.

Gold bracelets. Gold watches. Earrings galore!
People wishing happy tidings, and then, many more.

The year I finally got a bike. It was such a grand surprise.
I had just turned forty! I could hardly believe my eyes.

Snapshots of groups of people, gathered around my cake.
Me blowing out the candles, in one perfect 'take'!

The surprise vacations, and visitors from far away.
The many times something was done, to remember my day.

Then this year, my kids took me to visit Disney Land.
I laughed, ate, went on rides. Got soaking wet. It was grand!

I'm looking forward to next year, when my birthday comes
along.
No matter what happens, I know I'll hear my birthday song.

Because, although I had birthdays, that weren't so very great,
The ones I prefer to remember, have all been first rate!

I Haven't A Clue

I've put on some weight, to my great dismay.
I really don't know how I got this way.

My chin now has partners that sag and droop,
Can't possibly be caused by that tiny extra scoop.

My clothes don't fit. I blame it on the cleaners.
I refuse to believe that it's too many wieners.

Blouses I once wore, their buttons now pop.
I've begun wearing them as jackets, over a top.

My arms I keep covered with long billowy sleeves,
The material made up of the finest of weaves.

Slacks that I've worn at a length I adore,
I now find I have trouble. They don't reach the floor.

My hips it seems, have expanded some what,
Causing my pant legs to appear they've been cut.

Even my shoes have become unbearably tight
No room for my toes, on the left or the right.

How can I rid myself of this terrible blight?
Padlock the refrigerator? Keep food out of sight?

Well, that might work, but I'll not try it today.
I have company coming. What would they say?

My Age Group

I got up this morning, not much going on in my head.
I simply got up, and as usual, I made my bed.

It was then, in that usually undemanding act,
That I stumbled upon this effortless fact:

There are those in my age group, not able to make beds.
Can't tie their shoes, put on clothes, nor brush the hair on their
heads.

They can't run the vacuum, scrub the floors or even dust.
It takes all of their power to do the things that they must.

Their grandchildren they hug, but quite gingerly it's true.
It hurts even more, to help buckle their shoe.

They can't see as well, so reading a book is not fun.
They don't like rainy days, but don't dare go in the sun.

So I give special thanks this morning, as my chores I perform,
And promise not to complain that I'm too cold or too warm.

I've been blessed with good health, my whole life through,
And though I don't like chores, I'm glad these are things I can
still do.

He'll Help Us Through

We accept growing old, with it's aches and it's pains.
We even accept that death will come, and know of the gains.

But, we learn that a young person, still so much to give,
Is faced with a struggle, just to be able to live.

Why do we have cancers, blood disorders and such?
Did we achieve too little, or maybe failed too much?

We cry out for miracles, to save those we love.
We beg and implore, for help from above.

It just isn't fair! We cry at the assault.
How could this be? Where lies the fault?

But, then as this day closes, we realize what we need is to pray.
So down on our knees, in humbleness we say, "Give us this
Day..."

In our heart of hearts, we know that He always has a plan.
He will help us through. Ease our pain. Do whatever He can.

He understands the hurt and the grief. He gave His only son.
We understand all of this, too. "God's will be Done..."

Just Another Trip

A dear friend, many years ago, entertained me with stories,
Of her life during the Great Depression, (and its glories).

There were memories, of course, of no jobs and no food,
But, also light moments, when her little family found good.

The way neighbors helped neighbors sometimes in the dark
of night.
And how these same neighbors, were there to help when it
grew light

When her husband found work she traveled by train, beside
him to be,
The children were told to lie about their ages, so they could
ride free.

She told of many hardships, traveling from Texas to the west
coast
The love they had for each other. Of this they did boast.

They were on the road, for many years, just to make a living.
Through it all, they were fortunate, and were very thanks
giving.

Time went by, and their lives eventually took a sharp turn.
Their children went to college with the money they did earn.

Their golden years were now upon them. Many friendships
they did form.
I'll never forget our Saturday morning coffees, which became
the norm.

One such day, when we were together, she mentioned her greatest fear.
She was afraid of dying. Didn't want to leave those who were so dear.

I was stunned at this comment, as I saw the tears in her eyes.
Wanted to console her, as she thought of those last goodbyes.

I tried to explain to her, a simple truth, in a very simple mode.
We all must die someday. We must all go down that road.

That she was well prepared for it. She had traveled all her life.
It would be just another trip. This one would have no strife.

She seemed much relieved, as we continued our talk on that day.
It is just another trip. Each of us will learn to know the way.

Valentine's Day Blues

Do you know that today is Valentine's Day? A day for lovers.
But, I've never felt much a part of it. It just seems like all the
others.

Oh, I've sent my share of cards and gifts throughout the years,
But, usually I've sent them, while holding back some tears.

You see. I've never been in love, not once in all this time.
I've loved, wholeheartedly. But, it never was sublime.

I've read stories. Seen movies. Listened to romantic croons.
I've cried many unhappy tears, while singing my own woeful
tunes.

What is it like to love someone so deeply, that your own heart
bleeds?
That their very words become the breath your own body
needs.

I can't imagine it. I don't know how it can feel.
Can only look at someone else. See their head reel.

But, as I say these words, it's quite apparent to me,
That I am who I am, and I'm where I'm supposed to be.

Yes, I've had some lonely days and my share of lonely nights.
But, I never have big arguments, or even tiny fights.

I come and go, in my world, pretty much as I please.
And it's okay if I don't like my hamburgers with cheese.

I have loving children and grandchildren. A few true friends.
I know this wonderful circle of love, hasn't any frayed ends.

So when I look back on my life, to see if I've come very far.
I note that though I've never fallen in love, I've given it a bit of
a jar.

And I know I wouldn't trade my life, for any others that I've
seen
The grass on the other side of the fence, isn't really so green.

As this Valentine's Day comes to a close, I'm very glad I'm me.
Though I've never been in love, I thank God that love has been
in me.

Unconditional Love

It wasn't very long ago, I wrote a gloomy rhyme.
I was sort of blue. Should have picked a better time.

I was bemoaning that Valentine's Day was here.
Didn't feel there was anything worthwhile to cheer.

But, as I sat through that long evening all alone,
I remembered the calls I had received on the phone.

Tho' not exactly on that day, they certainly do matter.
My son, daughters, and grandchildren. How we do chatter.!

I haven't been in love, romantically. This is very true.
I've been in love, unconditionally. No reason to feel blue.

My children and my grandchildren taught me how to be in love.
I felt it the moment I saw them. These angels from above.

They give me inspiration. Help me to see the brighter side.
As I go through each day on earth, my heart is opened wide.

So I say 'thank you', to my family for teaching me the art,
Of sharing the wonderful feelings that I have in my heart.

The Great Love of My Life

If Jesus were to come here today,
I wonder what we'd do.
I know the very moment I see Him,
My heart will feel brand new.

The whole world will know He has come again.
The promise has been kept
People will rejoice and bow before Him.
Gone are the tears they wept.

Jesus will ask us, now to come with Him.
Leave all we know behind.
He'll take us to our Heavenly Father,
And loose the ties that bind.

For the promise made, is now before us.
He's brought us through the night.
If we've done our best, the reward will be,
Our soul will see God's light.

If Jesus were to come here today,
My face would glow with glee.
For Jesus is the great love of my life,
Today He sets me free!

The Blessings of Being Late

I was running late the other day, which I really hate to do.
But, I couldn't get my act together. My life was a zoo!

As I finally left my driveway, hurrying on my way,
I was held up by a traffic jam. This just wasn't my day.

When finally, I was on the road, I heard a siren's wail.
An accident just moments before, took the wind from my sail.

I was of course, held up again, from getting to my destination.
But as I sat there, awareness hit me, and I was ashamed of my
frustration.

The frightening thought was that the wailing siren might
have been for me,
Had I been on time, trying to be where I thought I needed to
be.

I've learned that, although I still try to get to my destinations
on time,
If by chance I'm held up for any reason, I'll try to think up a
rhyme.

But, the most significant point, is to count my blessings, as I sit
and wait.
There are many things more important, than worrying about
being late.

Morning In May

It's the first Monday in May,
And here I sit.
I don't know what I expected,
But this isn't it.

When thoughts come to me,
Of the lovely month of May,
I think of flowers and blue skies,
And the warmth of the day.

I think of children playing,
Yelling, and having pure fun.
Of gray-haired couples happily
Sharing a bench in the sun.

Birds chirping loudly in the trees,
Happy to be alive.
People working in offices,
Waiting for the stroke of five.

Instead, on this Monday,
The first in May,
The skies overhead are
Shrouded in gray.

The sun is not shining,
And it's not very warm.
No bees are out,
There's nary a swarm.

But, despite the outlook,
On this May morn,
I still have a smile,
And I am glad I was born.

I have an abundance of days,
To look forward to.
And the best part is that I,
Can share them with you.

Three O'clock Visitor

It was three o'clock in the morning, when
She suddenly awoke from slumber.
She opened her eyes and stared straight ahead.
Startled by what hovered above her.

It was a soft white, filmy appearing mass,
That seemed to float in the air.
She knew that she should probably get up,
But, too scared…she just lay there.

Thoughts racing through her frightened mind,
Of what it could possibly be.
Could her eyes be deceiving her?
The light was dim . She couldn't see.

She mustered up just enough courage,
To turn the bedside light on.
The moment that the light filled the room,
She looked up. The mass was gone.

After a while, she fell back to sleep.
Her alarm awoke her at Six.
She began preparing to face the day,
Deciding her mind had played tricks.

Two days later, a message left on her phone,
Informed her a friend passed away.
When she found out the rest of the story,
Was amazed at what they did say.

Her friend was taken to the hospital,
Two nights before, and did die.
It was three o'clock in the morning!
Did she stop in, to say goodbye?

Note: This actually happened to me. j.

Not After Three

Three o'clock in the morning, so I've been told,
Is the 'witching hour,' warned in days of old.
I don't know whether to believe it or not,
And I know it's not always right on the dot.

But, quite often around that time of the night,
I have awakened with a terrible fright.
My bed is shaking! I lay awake in fear.
I want to cry out, but there's no one to hear.

At other times when I've been awakened so,
I hear a noise, down in the basement below.
It's a tapping noise. A very steady beat.
I block the sounds with my head in the sheet.

And then there are times, there are things in the air.
So many of them, I do nothing but stare.
They seem to bounce off my walls! Won't settle down.
I get into my car. Take a ride downtown.

When I get back home, day is about to break.
I don't go back to bed. I'm now wide awake.
What should I do about this problem so rare?
Stay up all night? Or just nod off in a chair.

I think if I talk to my sister, or a friend,
One of them will help, with a shoulder to lend.
But, this is the answer that they gave to me,
"You can call anytime, just not after three!"

Christmas Goodwill

Christmas is very close, and the wonders of it fill my heart.
It always gives me an inner glow, right from the very start.

I look forward to seeing shoppers, as they go from store to store.
Looking for just the right gift, for each one that they adore.

I cheerfully check my mailbox, as I go from day to day.
Hoping to hear from close friends, and those who are far away.

Everyone seems cheerier and quicker to return a smile.
Makes me wish that Christmas could last longer than a while.

Why is it we can't seem to keep this feeling all year round?
Why do we just to dole it out, as if it comes by the pound?

It's always in our hearts. It sits there throughout the year.
It really shouldn't take a tree or a card to make it reappear.

I'm going to make a special effort, and my heart with happiness fill.
I'll greet each day of the New Year, with more than a little goodwill.

I'll say 'good morning' to those I meet, as they begin their day.
And keep a smile on my own face, as I go on my way.

As each day ends, I'll say my prayer, and be thankful for this life.
I'll ask God to please guide me, so that I may ease another's strife.

The Gift of Christmas

Christmas is here, and another year is drawing to a close.
We've all been waiting for Santa Claus and his "show of shows."

Our shopping is done, and our packages are wrapped.
Our homes are decorated and the tree, with a star is capped.

It seems that especially at this time of year,
Our thoughts lovingly turn to those we hold most dear.

Our family members, although some may be very far away,
Are closer in our hearts, with each "Merry Christmas," we say.

Our friends and acquaintances seem happier by far,
As their faces they turn up, to the shining Christmas Star.

The true meaning of Christmas, once again comes to this earth,
As we fill our hearts and homes, with happiness and mirth.

Wouldn't it be great if we could carry this feeling all year 'round?
To somehow, after the holiday, still hear the Christmas sound.

But, at least we can take a few moments to remember the reason,
That we were given the Gift of Gifts, during this wonderful season.

Our Christmas Club

We're going on a lovely weekend cruise,
A dear friend, my two sisters, and I.
We've been planning to get together
To celebrate Christmas in July.

We try to get together in December,
To celebrate our Dear Lord's Birth.
But, sometimes we're just not able.
Although, we surely know the worth

Being with loved ones is joyous.
It's a time we dearly adore.
We decided to celebrate Christmas
Each year, by simply adding one more.

We planned a gala weekend for July.
But, ran into a scheduling woe.
It we stuck to the date we had planned,
Some of us wouldn't be able to go.

We then changed the date to August,
And changed the venue, too.
Our Christmas in July is no longer then,
And our weekend will be on the blue.

We're already thinking of next Christmas,
Not the one in December, but July
The thought is that maybe we could plan
A balloon trip into the sky.

But, that would mean we'd have to change
The time again to comply.
They say balloon trips are not very good,
In the hot days of July.

Well, for now we'll just concentrate
On August, for our first Christmas in July.
We'll have such fun just being together.
We'll laugh, we'll reminisce and we'll cry.

Because being together during Christmas
Is a time we all adore.
We always loved that holiday so much,
And now, each year we'll have one more.

She's No Lady

The storm is coming, we've been told.
For this, we've put our lives on hold.

We've cleared our pictures from the walls,
Checked everything, from roof to halls.

Raised our possessions from the floor,
In case the water comes through the door.

Made trips to the store, getting food, nails and wood,
Plan to head out of town, as we know we should.

Bought batteries, water, even generators sometimes,
Nothing more to do, except make up these rhymes.

We think of those we love, those held most dear.
And in our hearts, we feel the gnawing of fear.

The storm is coming. It's Frances by name.
We know that much. We're not sure of her game.

She's out there, churning in the dark Atlantic,
Mere thoughts of her, causing such fear and panic.

Where will she go, this unpredictable Cyclops?
Will she meander onto our shores, or pull out all the stops?

You think of the name Frances. You picture sweet ladies.
But this is a monster, right out of Hades.

What have we done, to get her so riled?
She makes you think of a tamper-throwing child.

There's no reasoning with her. There's no relief.
She just keeps on coming, spewing her grief.

She gives no thought to property or life,
Shows no partiality to husband or wife.

The old, the infirmed must depend on others.
The little ones cling, wide eyed, to their mothers

And on she comes, this Frances of Hate.
As though she's obsessed, to keep this date.

Frances is coming, of that fact we're sure.
She won't be gentle. She's not demure.

She has already gained a reputation, bad.
It does us no good to get upset or mad.

We need to keep our minds and manners intact,
Although we know we're going to get sacked.

We must be prepared. That is the key.
We've been warned! She's coming by sea.

Send notes to your family and friends that you love,
Then say your prayers to the Lord above.

If you've done all you can to be safe and secure,
God will do the rest, of this you must be sure.

Now hold your loved ones close to your heart,
Turn off your electricity, lock your doors and depart.

Tomorrow will dawn with a blue sky so bright,
You will be grateful. You've made it through the night.

It's Our World

Tsunamis, blizzards, never ending rain.
We turn on the TV and hear only of pain.

Hurricanes, sinkholes and ruined crops.
People trying to save worldly goods. Wielding mops.

Flooding, mudslides, tornados from above.
What is going on in this world that we love?

Some say that it is God. He is not happy with us.
That we need to change our ways to gain His trust.

There are those who say that God is just being cruel,
That between Him and us, there is a duel.

Well, all of these notions are thought provoking,
But, maybe He just feels that our values need stoking.

God is not the cause of sadness, hardships and strife.
But, He is here to help us thorough it. Have joy in our life.

Possibly He wants us to again realize that He is the One,
Who will help us through, these days without sun.

He gave us a conscience, basic common sense and a brain.
Seems He would expect us to use these for our gain.

Maybe He wants us to understand, that nature is a force,
But, following His teachings should always be our course.

He gave us this world, to live in and enjoy. It was His gift.
The chaff from the grain we must learn to sift.

So although it seems that this earth is in devastation,
With our prayers and God's help, we will see our salvation.

Katrina's Wrath

I watch the news this morning and I am totally at a loss for words.
Hurricane Katrina has dealt a deadly blow to humanities hordes
People are devastated. Alone. No hope for a reprieve.
They can only look around at the destruction. And grieve.

No water to drink, nor to use to simply wash hands and faces.
No electricity. No gas. No food. No phones. Nothing in most cases.
Mile after mile of desolation, covered by mud, debris, and putrid water.
People looking for their lost relatives. Their son or daughter.

Others being chopped out of their attics, by rescue teams.
Water lapping at their heals. Searching with only flashlight beams.
Buildings completely collapsed from the wind and waters' weight.
The old and the young helplessly praying. Wondering of their fate.

Fires are erupting. There's no one coming to put them out.
People on rooftops, praying for help. Facing life with doubt.
The clothes on their back, now sum and total of all that they own.
Wondering what they must have done, to warrant the wrath now sown.

And now it's the second day. New Orleans is sinking into itself.
Water pouring through the breached levees. No one can help.
Twenty-five thousand people told to evacuate from the dome.
Texans opening their hearts and giving refuge. People can't go home.

Sand bags weighing three thousand pounds can't stop the flow.
People wandering the flooded roads, don't know where to go.
Some are looting the flooded stores, seeking basic needs.
The heat is stifling. The water is putrid. Sowing barbaric seeds.

Help is on the way, as Americans stand up to be counted.
National, State and Local levels are responding. Rescue is mounted.
Money is pouring in. Blood is being given. Hope is beginning to rise.
But, it will be many months before the fright is removed from victims' eyes.